AWAKENING

THE SIX

STEPS

TO

AWAKEN A NEW YOU

Julia Jean-Baptiste

Unless otherwise indicated, all Scripture quotations are taken from the King James Version of the Bible.

Awakening The Six Steps To Awaken A New You

Copyright © 2016

By Julia Jean-Baptiste

Published in the United States by Birds Eye View Publishing

ISBN: 978-0-998289403

Printed in the United States of America

PRESENTED TO:

_____

FROM:

_____

DATE:

_____

Contents

Foreword

One of the greatest discoveries that we can make in our lifetime, second to knowing God, is discovering who God has made us to be. Many persons live their entire lives, and never really touch the surface of finding out the 'who' and 'why' about themselves. This is very tragic because, a person who has an incorrect view of themselves through God's eyes, will have an incorrect view of the world around them, and everyone in it. The truth is, our external perception, is shaped by our internal conception. Another way of saying it is, the truth that we conceive about ourselves, is the guiding principle that directs our perception of everything and everyone around us.

How does one find their way to self-discovery, and living out the God-ideal? In this maze of countless other confused and disillusioned individuals, how does one make sense and find clarity amidst the chaos? What can we do to make each day count, and to make our lives resonate with purpose and joy? There is no easy answer. There are many that have tried on their own to fix their lives through humanistic, self-help efforts, and have only made it worse. What are the steps of turning a seemingly purposeless life, into a purposeful life? The author, in her very soft, yet strong way, outlines some very basic steps to jump-starting our lives, and creating the better future that God has ordained for each of us. In this riveting book, Julia has compiled simple, but yet profound principles, that can certainly offer an individual hope, and can steer them in the right direction.

I love the skillful way in which Julia combines Biblical principles, with the practical success stories from achievers of the past and the present. This powerful, easy read book offers just what we all need to bring our lives into alignment with God's design for our lives. I highly recommend this book to anyone who desires to bring quality, and purpose to their life. The 'Awakening' will truly awaken your spirit to recognize, and apply, the biblical truths that have been the hallmark of success for all those before who have applied them. Get ready for your journey to discovery. Read it, and LEAP!!!

Dr. Clement M. Neely

Senior Pastor

The Word Church

Nassau, Bahamas

"Trust God, He does not lie or change His mind. When He speaks He acts and His promises endure. His blessings over your life cannot be reversed. He has not planned misfortune and trouble for you, but He will redeem it. He is with those who proclaim Him their king as He brings you forth in strength.
Curses and magic cannot prevail against you. People will see His reflection in your life and declare His wonder. "

(Lisa Bevere)

(Numbers 23:19-23)

Introduction

In 2013, I had the great opportunity to attend "The Gathering" in Atlanta, Georgia. This powerful life changing event allowed me to come face to face with some great men and women of the faith of whom I had only heard or read about. However, prior to this event, there was this one speaker who, I had never heard of.

Her name was Ms. Lisa Bevere. As she came on stage, I just knew that this was a woman that I wanted to know more about. Her posture! Her voice! Her energy! Yes, she commanded her environment, and it spoke volumes to me.

After her session was over, I bought so many of the items that were at her table. One book in particular that I picked up and knew I needed to read was Lioness Arising, Wake Up and Change Your World.

If I told you that I immediately read the book, I would not be telling the truth. Throughout the remainder of the conference, I picked up so many great reading materials from others like Jimmy Evans, Andrew Wommack, and John Maxwell.

Upon my arrival home, I picked up and began what I thought was a dive into Ms. Bevere's book. Yet, before I could get to the heart of the book, I found myself stopping at the beginning where I believe Ms. Bevere strategically placed Numbers 23:19-23.

After reading this verse, I literally found myself stuck right there. I was so mesmerized by the words on the page. It was as though the words leaped off the page and spoke to every fibre of my being.

After the tragic loss of my mother, I found it very hard to connect to the God that I grew up learning about. I literally can say that for some time I became an atheist. For over a year, I wanted nothing to do with this God who I believed took my mom.

Yet, he didn't give up on me even when I had given up on him. The God of my mother found a way to bring me back home. During my time back, I literally had to put my trust in him to live from one day to the next. Over the years, my walk with him has been nothing short of amazing. He surprises me daily by what he has and continues to do in my life. He has strengthened me in my weakness and over and over again showed me that no evil shall prevail against me. His blessing on my life continues to show how being allowed to be in the fiery furnace and coming out with a few bruises is still a reflection of his love. His finished work causes rest. If he did it for me, he has and can do it for you. AWAKEN to the life that has been waiting for you!

"And be not conformed to this world; but be ye transformed by the renewing of your mind, that ye may prove what is that good, and acceptable, and perfect, will of God."

-Romans 12:2, KJV-

STEP ONE:

Allow your impossibilities to become your possibilities!

Mark 10:27 says, *"And Jesus looking upon them saith, with men it is impossible, but not with God: for with God all things are possible."*

In my own life, as a believer, there are many verses, the latter being one of them, that I have heard and even recited on many occasions over and over again. Yet, in gaining honesty and clarity with myself and God, at this season of my life, I can truly say that I have not truly embraced nor have I applied its true meaning to my life. Hebrews 11:1 is also another one of those verses, "Now faith is the substance of things hoped for and the evidence of things not seen." What does that mean? In seeking an answer to that question, the Lord provided a quote from one of the greatest philosophers of his time, Albert Einstein. Einstein states, "imagination is everything. It is the preview of life's coming attractions. Imagination is more important than knowledge." Ok, so again I ask, what does that mean? Well for this answer, the Lord took me to another influential thinker of his time Sir Sigmund Freud. According to Freud, "dreams represent a disguised fulfillment of a represented wish." He believed that studying dreams provided the easiest road to the understanding of the unconscious activities of the mind. In search of finding the truth to the statement made by Freud, I was led to visit the life of an African-American whose life depicted the power of dreams. Dr. George Washington Carver who has been credited for being a humble, God fearing man who credited all his successes to his creator. During his life, Dr. Carver became a sought after and respected Scientist, Inventor, and Teacher who understood the power of dreams. In his biography, an illustration was shared of a young Carver who wanted a pocketknife. So without any money, the young Carver chose to ask God to send him one. While asleep, the young Carver was shown in a dream the location of the knife. In his dream, the pocketknife was shown as sticking out of a watermelon. After awakening from his dream, the young Carver went to the very spot where he had seen the melon and in it was the pocket knife that he had asked God for.

The following illustration was one of many accounts of where Dr. Carver asked and in his dream received an answer. Such dreams provided him with the instructions to the invention of peanut milk, peanut butter and many more peanut products that gave him the name "Peanut Man."

In my own life, while growing up on a small island, some of my greatest challenges have been in bridging the gap between what is and what can be. I remember reading a story about a young lady who grew up in the heart of New York City. It appeared as though all the odds seemed stacked up against her. In this story, the young teenager had a family that was completely dysfunctional. Her mom, when she wasn't strung out on drugs, was on the streets as a prostitute. Her dad was an alcoholic who found himself not able to hold down a job for longer than the wind blew across the room, and her siblings were never able to do much of anything together except argue and be disrespectful. Her life was one that seemed like it was over before it even begun. Yet, at some point in her life faith allowed her to cross path with a woman who saw something in her that she didn't see in herself. Faith is the substance of things hoped for and the evidence of things not seen. This woman who miraculously came into her life went on to introduce this young girl to a life where happiness almost seemed possible. She provided her with a part-time job where she was able to care for her pets, at her home. Melissa did such an amazing job at the tasks given to her that the woman started to invest more and more time into helping her create a new image about the possibilities, for her life. She began sharing pictures and stories of places she had visited around the world. One particular picture was on a remote private island in the Caribbean, an island owned by one person. After sharing more and more of her pictures, Melissa admitted that she had never known that such beautiful places truly existed. The more the woman continued sharing amazing parts of her life with Melissa the more she started realizing that her present reality might not have to dictate her future. Slowly, Melissa started to shift the projection of her life. She began to understand that the potential for her life was endless.

Melissa went on to work some other pet gigs, saved her money, became a first generation post graduate and later went on to pass her state bar exam. Despite all of her obstacles, Melissa was able to obtain "Success Against the Odds," first in her way of thinking and then in her strategic actions. Melissa's story provided an account that neither social, economic status or geographic location should be a determining factor for you not to live a successful and significant life. Your ability to move beyond the limiting beliefs of your mind is only subject to the excuses created by you. Melissa's ability to release her faith moved her from one realm to the next.

"But without faith, it is impossible to please him: for he that cometh to God must believe that he is, and that he is a rewarder of them that diligently seek him" (Hebrews 11:6). In my own life, I have had to learn how to start truly, thinking and living outside the box. So in you seeking to release the limits off your thinking and to begin moving to that place where dreams become possible, you too will have to learn how to, "cooperate with your dreams" (Pastor Storey) if you are going to change the outcome of your life. You will now have to learn how to become intentional about living a purpose driven life. A life where you will have to strategize to win.

As you may have already experienced in your own life and as you witnessed in Melissa's story, the road to living your dreams will not be easy. The tests will come, and the challenges may be severe. Yet, the secret to withstanding the impossibilities of life is to become rooted and grounded in the love of God. It is coming to a greater awareness that no matter how often the turmoil of life seeks to shake, rattle or roll you around your foundation is based on the finished work of God. God needs you to be strategic about using knowledge, faith and action to move in the direction of living an abundant, passion and purpose driven life. Go ahead! Live your dream and get ready to SOAR!

Step One: Key Points

- Identify your passion and follow your dream!

- Conduct research around your passion!

- Identify the prerequisites around your passion!

- Take necessary steps to develop your passion!

- Work your passion!

Exercise 1

1. What inspires you?

2. What dreams have you been suppressing?

3. What experiences, gifts, or talents do you have to make your dreams come true?

Quote:

"The greatest pleasure in life is doing things people said you cannot do."

(Walter Bagehot)

_____

_____

_____

_____

_____

_____

_____

_____

_____

_____

_____

_____

_____

_____

_____

_____

_____

"And be not conformed to this world; but be ye transformed by the renewing of your mind, that ye may prove what is that good, and acceptable, and perfect, will of God."

-Romans 12:2, KJV-

STEP TWO:

Work Towards Your Purpose!

John 17:4 says, *"I have glorified You on the earth. I have finished the work which You have given Me to do."*

As seen in John 17:4, Jesus was sent to glorify and finish the work that was given him. Therefore, as an ambassador for the Kingdom, your work is "to discover and become what you were created to be through self-manifestation" (Dr. Myles Munroe). When God created you, he took his time and sculpted a masterpiece. God created you as a one of a kind priceless jewel. Did you know that in the world there are only four gemstones that are classified as precious because of their historical importance and value? In her book, The Undiscovered Jewel, Author Dell Scott does an amazing job of helping her readers understand about one of those jewels. Dell helps her readers understand the "exhausting process that a diamond travels, to become that perfect gem." As a diamond is being transformed to reach its finished state, it will have to go through so many stages before it is approved. Man of God, Woman of God, the moment that you accepted God into your life, just like a diamond, you have been approved to do great works. As you read about the uniqueness of the last three gems, you should begin to recognize that your value is great and that your uniqueness separates you to do what you born to do. The sapphire has also been classified as one of the four precious gemstones in the world. "Due to their natural hardness, they are extremely durable and are said to represent truth, sincerity, and consistency." When God chose you to carry out his purpose, on earth, he knew that like the sapphire you would have to be endued with certain traits that would allow you to complete his assignment or work given to you. Like the sapphire, you have been equipped. Red is the color of the Ruby. Its color is the most important quality of this precious gemstone.

In the Indian culture, the Ruby is known to be the stone of Kings. Its color has been deemed a never-ending flame that creates passion and fire within. In order for you to complete the work given to you, you must do it with a level of passion that only comes from within. The final of the most precious gemstone is the Emerald. Emeralds are amongst the oldest gemstones in the world. Emeralds were created when a shift by plate tectonic moved the elements together. Emeralds typically contain inclusions that are visible to the unaided eye; these inclusions occur because of the intense pressure and its environment. Just like the Diamond, Ruby, Sapphire, and Emerald, "you possess the 4C's: "A specific cut, a unique color, a rare clarity, and a specific karat weight." In Romans 8:28, it states that, "all things work together for good to them that love God, to them who are the called according to his purpose." God has purposed you for such a time as this, and as his precious gem you must make up in your mind and heart that the battle belongs unto the Lord. Jesus has already won the victory. All you have to do is be mindful because the adversary of darkness, on earth, will not provide you with a free pass to fulfill your purpose. Your purpose should be something you are passionate about. So, make up your mind to fight the good fight of faith, knowing that, "God has not given us the spirit of fear; but of power, and of love, and of a sound mind" (2 Timothy 1:7 KJV).

Step Two: Key Points:

- Your purpose is to glorify God!

- Stop concentrating on who hurt, left or rejected you!

- God is for you and he loves You!

- Go before God and ask him for forgiveness from self and others!

- Ask God to direct and order your path!

- Trust God not man!

Exercise 2

1. Have you ever thought about what your purpose is?

2. Who will benefit as a result of you fulfilling your purpose?

3. How would you feel when in the middle of meeting your purpose you realize that your provisions have been met?

Quote:

"Choice not chance determines destiny"

(Aristotle).

———————————————————————

———————————————————————

———————————————————————

———————————————————————

———————————————————————

———————————————————————

———————————————————————

———————————————————————

———————————————————————

———————————————————————

———————————————————————

———————————————————————

———————————————————————

———————————————————————

———————————————————————

"And be not conformed to this world; but be ye transformed by the renewing of your mind, that ye may prove what is that good, and acceptable, and perfect, will of God."

-Romans 12:2, KJV-

STEP THREE:

Align yourself with those who are wise!

Luke 6:39-40 says, *"Can the blind lead the blind? shall they not both fall into the ditch? The disciple is not above his master: but every one that is perfect shall be as his master."*

Wow! As you just read, the word of God is very clear about aligning yourself with those who have more wisdom, knowledge, and understanding than you. If your dream is to make a great positive impact in your world and the world of others, you will have to align yourself and partner with others who are wiser and more driven than you. You will have to learn how to align yourself with others whose dreams are being played out before your eyes, and who have chosen to play big. In order to do great things, you will have to learn how to stand behind and follow great people. The best leaders were once the best followers. At times, for various reasons, you may not have direct access to those who have traveled and surpassed your goal, so be creative about being mentored. It may mean you have to become uncomfortable and choose to become an avid reader. It may also mean that you will have to learn technology and watch clips on YouTube. But whatever you do, you must do it with an intentional mindset. In my own journey to seek wisdom from those who are wise, I have invested, over a ten-year period, upwards of $50,000 to be in the room with great men and women who are experts or gurus in their area of discipline. I have had the pleasure of being in the room with Mr. Steve Harvey and his beautiful wife, Marjorie Harvey. I was able to hear and see first-hand that they are passionate about living a life that makes them happy but also doing it to demonstrate to others that success and a significant life is possible for those who are willing to work hard enough to achieve it. A little over a year ago, I traveled for the first time to California to be at a Motivating the Masses event with none other than the renowned exceptional speaker Ms. Lisa Nichols. While in her presence, she poured words upon words of encouragement and motivation into my life that has helped me to birth this book. I am honored that you are now reading it. My most recent investment was a trip that I took to Orlando, Florida to receive my International Certification that now makes me a Certified John Maxwell Trainer, Speaker, and Coach. The three-day intensive training often started at eight o'clock in the morning and concluded at eight o'clock at night. At this training, I was able to learn from not only the founders of the company, but I was able to learn, collaborate and gain knowledge from my JMT colleagues and family. As communication has the power to save a life, a selected number of JMT members have decided to continue our relationship where we are excited about pouring words of life into each other in hopes of helping to move us to a greater life of intentional living. How much better to get wisdom than gold! And to get understanding is to be chosen rather than silver! How powerful are those words from the richest and wisest man that ever lived?

Step Three: Key Points:

- Create your circle with people who have or are making a positive difference, in your life, community, or the world!

- Set clear short and long term goals that you and others can measure!

- Be willing to be intimidated by the brilliance of others in the room!

- Be around people who are humble, creative, bold, confident, assertive, diligent and courageous!

- If you don't have any positive influence in your life right now, you have a responsibility to go out for them!

- Soaring Eagles, Roaring Lions or Lioness'. Steve Harvey says, "No one builds anything of any great magnitude alone."

- Develop a teachable spirit that will serve you and others!

- Know that growth is often at a cost!

- Be willing to implement the nuggets from the wise!

Exercise 3

1. What organization can you partner with to reach your goals?

2. Who must you build a partnership with to help you to fulfill the given unique to you?

3. Do you have a mentor or coach that can help you on this journey?

Quote:

"Humility is one of the qualities often left out of the "self-made" man"

(Unknown)

_____

_____

_____

_____

_____

_____

_____

_____

_____

_____

_____

_____

_____

_____

_____

"And be not conformed to this world; but be ye transformed by the renewing of your mind, that ye may prove what is that good, and acceptable, and perfect, will of God."

-Romans 12:2, KJV-

STEP FOUR:

Keep moving forward!

Philippians 3:14 says, *"I press toward the mark for the prize of the high calling of God in Christ Jesus."*

Have you ever been in a situation where one tragedy ended and before you could catch your breath another one began? Yes, the distractions will come, and the commitments of life will continue. Yet, as they come, remember the key is to go through them. I implore you to remain steadfast, unmovable, always abounding in the work of the Lord, according to **1 Corinthians 15:58**. For you see, you have been given an assignment by the Creator, and that particular assignment, whatever it may be, is unique only to you. Rest assured that your abilities, talents, setups and setbacks were all given a stamp of approval from God himself. Had the greater one not given a thumbs up, you would have never been allowed to go through that fiery furnace. In the book of Job, God allowed all of Job's destructions to take place around him. However, the enemy was given specific instructions about not allowing any of the trials and tribulations to cause the death of God's servant. As it was with Job, so it shall be with you. God allowed Job to go through his adversities, and so shall it be with you. But remember to always keep your heart and eyes focused on the Lord. The Merriam-Webster dictionary defines, focus as, "a state or condition permitting clear perception or understanding. "Right here and right now, I charge you to let go of all those distractions and make a conscious decision to replace them with a commitment to always press towards your God-given destiny. God needs you to brush yourself off, pick up the broken pieces, put on the armor of God and continue to fight the good fight of faith. For it is in your decision to move forward, that you will realize that events once looked upon as failures were actually setups to move you closer to your purpose. In growing up, I was taught as probably many of you that there was no success in failure. Yet, I have learned most recently from many of my mentors, John Maxwell being one that there is a great accomplishment that takes place from failure. In one of his books, he notes that "success is a product of well-managed losses and defeats." Additionally, Albert Einstein stated that, "A person who never made a mistake never tried anything new." Let me take the time to explain from an example in my own life. About two years ago, I made a decision to quit my job as a Career Specialist. Over the last year of being in this area, I no longer was able to account for how I was able to impact the lives of the students that I had vowed to make an impact in their lives. Based on the governmental bureaucracy, I saw myself and the services I was asked to provide as a series of strings waiting to be pulled and not for the right reasons. So, without a true plan in place but for the sake of my sanity I quit. It would have been better if I had allowed them to fire me, that way I would have been able to walk away and be able to collect an unemployment check. Yet, it wasn't even about the money. It was about me not being able to truly add the kind of value that I knew that my students deserved. So, here I was without a plan and a job. Yet, the society and even I for a while deemed that as a less than power move and even went as far as labeling it as a complete failure. Yet, as I awoke from that daunting experience, I came out with a greater awareness about my why. I was able to answer the question of why I didn't need to keep myself trapped in a place where I was unable to move forward and establish a potential for myself and others. As I struggled through that very difficult part of my life, I knew I needed more help than I could provide for myself just through self- encouragement. Therefore, I started taking more power moves that led me to invest in not one but two amazing coaches. They allowed me to gain greater clarity about the next steps that would lead me towards my success. I knew that I needed help to move forward and chose to invest in me. I read somewhere that we learn the most from our failures. As I am on my second business with greater knowledge and wisdom about what I need to do to succeed, I would have to agree with that hard but true statement. I am now on my second business, and I have decided to move forward to live a life towards a greater calling. Fear is a feeling that successful people must overcome in order to become successful. Did you know that the fear of failure is mainly derived from the lack of mentoring and coaching? Yes, I failed once in business or so I thought, but what I have learned is that failure is a part of the success process. The good thing about lessons learned is that once you learn them, it is hard for you to repeat them again. My new community of mentors and coaches has now placed me in a position to win. As you continue to go on this journey with me, I hope this book will inspire you to find your why to JUMP!

Step Four: Key Points:

- Don't let fear and procrastination stop you!

- Step out in faith! Stay alert! Stay focus! John 10:10 states, "The enemy came to steal kill and destroy!" Him and his deceptive angels, aren't playing fairly so you shouldn't either!

- Be intentional about your future!

- Live in the present!

- Only look back to see how far you come

- Be very clear in writing your vision for the next chapter of your life. Lisa Nichols states, "the next chapter can be changed because we are still holding the pen."

- Be tenacious in writing your power statement that will help you daily to stay motivated for the next awesome chapters of your life!

- Be ok with failing forward

Exercise 4

1. Why do you need to move forward?

2. What goals will you accomplish in the next 60 days?

3. How will your life look different as you keep moving forward?

Quote:

"Feed your faith, and your doubts will starve to death"

(Les Brown).

_____

_____

_____

_____

_____

_____

_____

_____

_____

_____

_____

_____

_____

_____

_____

"And be not conformed to this world; but be ye transformed by the renewing of your mind, that ye may prove what is that good, and acceptable, and perfect, will of God."

-Romans 12:2, KJV-

STEP FIVE:

Every step will move you closer to accomplishing your purpose!

Psalms 37:23 says, *"The steps of a good man are ordered by the Lord: when he delights in his way."*

As you begin to step into your predetermined and predestined purpose, it won't be easy, but the word of God states that it will be well worth it. At this point, you should have started to put your strategic plan in place for living a purpose driven life. If you've started, I applaud you. If you haven't, I encourage you to get started, now! In building on your strategic plans, you should also adopt some power moves.

The first power move should be to become an organizer. If you are like most people, you are holding on to outdated receipts, newspapers, magazines, check books, bank statements and utility bills since grade school. I must admit that I have been very guilty of the latter; yet, in my quest to retrain my mind I had to realize that this clutter was a part of what was holding me back. In order for you to move towards your purpose, you will have to organize or even get rid of the clutter.

The second power move will be referred to as the purging process. It is the ability to purge yourself of religious thinking and replace it with relationship thinking. Religion has been formed around denomination, but relationship is formed around fellowship with God. At this point, learn how to spend time, for yourself, reading the word of God and listening to him speak to you. In your finances, purge yourself of unfruitful spending patterns and replace it with being a good steward of your money. It should become a habit to pay God with your tithes and pay yourself first. In health, purge yourself of unhealthy eating habits and replace it with a healthy lifestyle. During the course of your day, replace a candy bar with a fruit or small salad. The third power move in this section is focused on you becoming intentional about using a calendar to schedule your month, day and year. The fourth power move you will have to make is one that is vital to your success. For every small success that you make, you must learn how to celebrate. I can tell you that by default it is easier said than done. However, you need always to remember that God is always watching and cheering you on. So, take some time to cheer yourself on. The fifth power move is based on one word, commitment. In making the most of every step that you will ever take, make up your mind to do whatever it takes, as is moral and ethical. According to Merriam-Webster Dictionary, commitment is a promise to be loyal to someone or something. Unlike the previous sections, where the focus was more on you, this move that you must make should also be about others. If you have not figured it out yet, you need to know that your life and only your life may hold the key to helping unlock the potential within someone else. Yet, I caution you to recognize and realize that you cannot force anyone into something they don't want. God has given you the mandate to serve the world with your message, but he is only asking that you offer the gift of choice. In paying close attention and using the power of discernment, you will know you can only help those who are ready to be helped. This power step will lead you to a happier and healthier life for yourself and others. The last and probably the most important power move will always be the ultimate game changer. Be thankful and grateful to those who have helped you step into your greatness, and always seek to "Pay It Forward." If you are going to see any significant changes in the next chapter of your life, it is imperative for you to not only create and learn a new blueprint but become skillful at implementing it. The structure and framework of your new blueprint must speak to who you want to become so that you can speak it into existence until it becomes your reality. Remember this: Every opportunity you have to make someone else's dream come true will be a star for you.

Step Five: Key Points

- Let the method to your madness, work for and not against you.

- Be the person who will demonstrate to yourself that your steps have been ordered by the Lord.

- In celebrating your wins, it can be as simple treating yourself to Cold Stone or as elaborate as a cruise to the Bahamas.

- "Be the change you wish to see in the world" (Mahatma Gandhi).

Exercise 5

1. What behaviors will you have to let go of to step into your new you?

2. How will you reward yourself after your micro win?

3. How will you know when you have won?

Quote:

"If your compassion does not include yourself, it is incomplete"

(Gautama Buddha).

_____

_____

_____

_____

_____

_____

_____

_____

_____

_____

_____

_____

_____

_____

_____

_____

"And be not conformed to this world; but be ye transformed by the renewing of your mind, that ye may prove what is that good, and acceptable, and perfect, will of God."

-Romans 12:2, KJV-

STEP SIX:

Never take NO for an answer!

2 Corinthians 1:20 says, *"For all the promises of God in him are yea and in him Amen, unto the glory of God by us."*

The word says that you are to seek first the Kingdom of Heaven so that all things shall be added unto you. Yeah and amen, are the promises of God. If God has said it, then that settles it. So, settle in your mind that you serve a big God whose picture for your success is bigger than your big picture of success, but he needs you to trust the step by step process and simply answer YES!

Step Six: Key Points

- Yes, to walking in love!

- Yes, to spending time in the word!

- Yes, to living by faith!

- Yes, to the finish work that causes rest!

- Yes, to tithing!

- Yes, to worshiping and praising God!

- Yes, to Kingdom Living!

Exercise 6

1. Who will benefit from your answer of yes to God? List five people.

2. How important is it for you to finish your race?

3. What legacy will you leave behind?

Quote:

Psalms 85:12 says, *"Yea, the Lord shall give that which is good; and our land shall yield her increase."*

_____
_____
_____
_____
_____
_____
_____
_____
_____
_____
_____
_____
_____
_____
_____

Final Thoughts

(REPITITION BRINGS FORTH THE VISION) **Roman 12:2**

"And be not conformed to this world: but be ye transformed by the renewing of your mind, that ye may prove what is that good, and acceptable, and perfect, will of God."

Rescue can only come from the heart of those who want to be rescued! Join me in Your Rescue To Develop Your Best YOU!

"The greatest tragedy in life is not death, but a life without purpose."

Dr. Myles Munroe

LOVE YOURSELF!

Scriptures

May the scripture verses that tie in with those you have already read continue to bless you and move you from faith to FAITH!

Psalms 35:27- *"Let them shout for joy, and be glad, that favour my righteous cause; yea, let them say continually. Let the Lord be magnified, which hath pleasure in the prosperity of his servant."*

1 Timothy 6:17- *"Charge them that are rich in this world, that they be not highminded, nor trust in uncertain riches, but in the living God, who giveth us richly all things to enjoy."*

1 Thessalonians 1:3- *"Remembering without ceasing your work of faith, and labour of love, and patience of hope in our Lord Jesus Christ, in the sight of God and our Father."*

John 4:34- *"Jesus saith unto them, my meat is to do the will of him that sent me, and to finish his work."*

Philippians 3:12- *"Not as though I had already attained, either were already perfect: but I follow after, if that I may apprehend that for which also I am apprehended of Christ Jesus."*

Philippians 3:13- *"Brethren, I count not myself to have apprehended: but this one thing I do, forgetting those things which are behind, and reaching forth unto those things which are before.*

Proverbs 22:4- *"By humility and the fear of the Lord are riches, and honour, and life."*

Romans 12:1- *"I beseech you therefore brethren, by the mercies of God, that ye present your bodies a living sacrifice, holy acceptable unto God, which is your reasonable service."*

Psalms 1:3- *"And he shall be like a tree planted by the rivers of water, that bringeth forth his fruit in his season, his leaf also shall not wither; and whatsoever he doeth shall prosper."*

Deuteronomy 6:5- *And thou shalt love the Lord thy God with all thine heart, and with all thy soul, and with all thy might."*

Hebrews 4:9- *There remaineth therefore a rest to the people of God."*

Hebrews 4:3- *"For we which have believed do enter into rest, as he said, As I have sworn in my wrath, if they shall enter into my rest: although the works were finished from the foundation of the world."*

2 Timothy 4:7- *"I have fought a good fight, I have finished my course, I have kept the faith."*

Acknowledgements

Thanks goes out to Abba for giving me this opportunity to expand my ability to begin to live a life of impossibilities that will help to serve others. Although they are no longer with me, I would like to thank my awesome parents who used the Bible as the foundation to teach me about respect and compassion. I greatly acknowledge the love and support of my amazing husband William and daughter Kizia. I recognize and acknowledge Pastor Ronald D. Walker for providing the platform for an in-depth study of the word. I also would like to thank all the men and women who over the past two years were instrumental in molding my decision to begin and finish this project and to many others who, over the course of my life developed my character.

Special Thank You to my 2015 **AWAKENING TEAM**: Dr. Kishma George, Diva Dell, Evangelist Trina Bowers, Dr. Hakeem Collins and Dr. Naim Collins!

Thank You to Rev. Seaton Wilson

Special Thank You to Mr.Prosper!

Sources

Bevere, Lisa. (2011). "Lioness Arising. Messenger International.,

Michael, Burgen. (2007). "George Washington Carver: Scientist, Inventor, and Teacher." Books.Google.com, Web.

Scott, L. Dell. (2014). The Undiscovered Jewel. Threefold Publishing.,

The Holy Bible, KJV. Bible.com, YouVersion, LLC, 2010 Web.

"Gemstone Guide, Precious Gemstones," hsn.com, HSN LLC, 2016 Web.

About the Author

I feel confident saying that my life story has seemed to have been one that came straight out of the most popular book in the world. And I am honored to use my setbacks and comebacks to help you release the power in you. **POWER** in obedience. Life is made up of a series of chapters, and you can't get stuck in any one chapter! After much spiritual searching, prayers from loving individuals, and my coaches, I am able to embrace this mantra and make every day of my life intentional.

My passion for making my community a better place for our children, elderly, and those who must live and visit the Virgin Islands of the United States led me to announce my candidacy to run for governor of the USVI. My run was guided towards "being the change you wish to see in the world." It was a stand to encourage others to become more involved and responsible civic citizens. Over the years, I have earned three degrees that have taken me from one level of growth to the next. I have completed certificates in areas like Project Management that was never an area of interest. Life is a book of chapters where you can't get stuck!

In this journey of life, I lost my mother, at the age of fifty-two, to cancer and my father, one day, before his birthday. I have had to quit a profession that became spiritually and physically unhealthy, due to external and internal factors. I have opened and closed a boutique that greatly reduced my financial structure. Yes, I was unable to secure my candidacy for governor. Yet, through it all I couldn't afford to get stuck in any one of my life.

Today as a proud mother and wife, I have learned the power of listening to that still small voice as my guide. That voice led me to be a Lisa Nichols Abundance Now Ambassador, a Steve Harvey SOAR Academy student, and a John Maxwell International Certified Coach, Speaker, and Trainer. I am currently a business owner who continues to move towards my purpose driven life of serving others and reaching towards spiritual wholeness and an intentional life of purpose.

Author's Picture

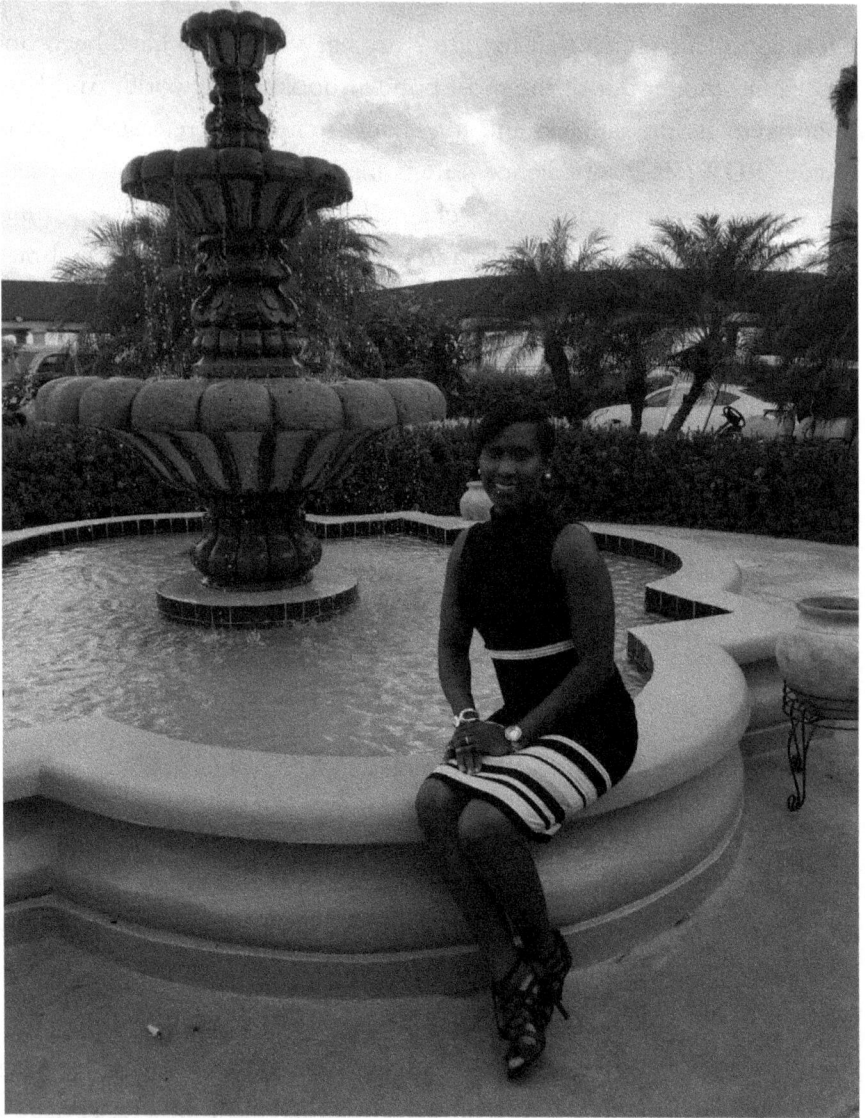

THANK YOU!

Art of Communication

What were the greatest nuggets that you came away with after reading this book? How will you use them to **SOAR?**

_____

_____

_____

_____

_____

_____

_____

_____

_____

_____

_____

_____

_____

_____

_____

_____

(The author would love to hear from you about how this book Inspired YOU)! And please share a review on amazon.com

Contact: wopusvi@gmail.com

Additional copies of this book are available at www.amazon.com, www.womenofpowerusvi.com, and other book distributors.

Julia resides in the beautiful Virgin Island of the United States with her family.

For Future Speaking engagements:

For Individual Coaching:

For Mastermind Building:

www.womenofpowerusvi.com

wopusvi@gmail.com

1-571-623-9365

BIRDS EYE VIEW PUBLISHING

(We bring your story to the World)!

www.birdseyeviewpublishing.com

JOHN 3:16

"For God so loved the world, that he gave his only begotten Son, that whosoever believeth in him should not perish, but have everlasting life."

CELEBRATE

YOUR

AWAKENING!!!

www.ingramcontent.com/pod-product-compliance
Lightning Source LLC
Chambersburg PA
CBHW071642050426
42443CB00026B/938